My Dream....My Heart ....My Moment

William Randy Parker Jr.

authorHOUSE®

AuthorHouse™
1663 Liberty Drive
Bloomington, IN 47403
www.authorhouse.com
Phone: 1-800-839-8640

First published by AuthorHouse   3/14/2011

ISBN: 978-1-4567-5100-5 (e)
ISBN: 978-1-4567-5101-2 (sc)

Library of Congress Control Number: 2011904480

Printed in the United States of America

Any people depicted in stock imagery provided by Thinkstock are models, and such images are being used for illustrative purposes only. Certain stock imagery © Thinkstock.

This book is printed on acid-free paper.

Contents

Together

Hand and hand

Our love continues to stand

Putting words down

Without making a sound

What is all around?

In my mind is a lovely sound

It's like a press room

So many questions going around

My hearts in good hands

Cause she knows where I stand

Books

So much information in them

Words can't help them

Going on and on

As each page turns along

Feels like it's going to take it slow

Just one look

Can have you feel hooked

There is so much you can learn

But my love for you will never be on the run

Just To Hear It

From the most beautiful person

That has so much love within

Makes my day brighter everyday

When I see her walk this way

Always on my mind

Not a second goes by

Such a good heart

I have loved her from the start

Big Mouth

She knows who she is

Ain't even got to say who it is

The sweetest woman I know

That always keeps me on my toes

She knows just what to say

I close my eyes and everything goes away

The love of my life

Right here on my right side

Lay It Down

Those three words

Can often be heard

Flowing off the persons lips

Feels like their body is doing flips

In another world

Cause there is nothing to tell

As the body of hers lays there

She tells you with her eyes you gave it well

Put It Down

Have you going on circles

But there is nothing there to help you

Mind blowing it may have been

But could you take what was within

As deep as the passion went

Almost felt like it was heaven sent

All the way in your love

Never felt like coming up

To stay down

Until someone has the rounds

Look at me

You can tell I want you

But it's on you with what you want to do

We can just lay there

While I play in your hair

I don't know what to say

But I'm glad you came my way

So much love we can make

I am beyond words to say

Just thinking about you

How much I really missed you

Waiting

So much time passes

With you the love I have within

To be able to kiss you

I can't wait to hear from you

The way your body feels

I can always tell you are near

Always on my mind

Cause there is so much time

Waiting for you I will

The love for you I really feel

Starting Point

It's so much I want to do with you

That's how much I miss you

A masterpiece you are

How you have stole my heart

To be in really good hands

I know where I stand

She has opened my eyes

Bought so much love back inside

So come and go with me

Trust that you will see me

Seeing you smile

Nothing can take that away

Makes my heart feel a certain way

Seeing the joy on your face

Makes me say how is my baby feeling this way

When it all comes down

Makes me turn that frown upside down

That love that she has

Makes me forget about the past

Her love is something that will last

Makes me say what the present and future has

Being with you

Having you so close

Always making the most

Clapping cause I am happy

That she decided to look inside me

To separate the good from the bad

Accepting what I had

To show unconditional love

Even if it is a hug

Emotions sometimes fly

But from your love I will never hide

Down on me

Slowing the pace down

Looking at you up and down

Having your on mind

Without letting you know what is going on inside

Licking your lips

You think you know what it is

Have a creative mind

Makes you want to put that cd on rewind

Breaking this moment down

The use of 5 senses is about to go down

5 Senses

Can be used at any time

Depending what's on someone's mind

Having control

Not letting your mind be on a roll

Wondering how something is

But to be careful not to miss

How will that person feel?

When it's right in front of them

As the beat plays along

What are senses will be when alone

William Randy Parker Jr. - 13

Struggles

Seem to come like everyday

Makes you want to turn away

Your heart feels like glass

Wondering how long it will last

Not feeling that good

Not knowing what to do

Feeling like wanting to cry

When will the pain go to the side?

Time

Spending it with someone special

That will be there to help you

Being at your lowest point

When you need someone the most

Not feeling good enough

To put up with all this stuff

Trying to make it day by day

Knowing that your ship will soon sail away

William Randy Parker Jr. - 15

Words

They can sometimes hurt

Some can make your heart melt

Not looking for excuses

But the damage has moved in

Holding on to see what will happen

To get rid of all the sad words from within

Expressions are up and down

But an apology can't be found

Book Bag

Can contain many items

Do we try to hide them?

We carry it on our shoulders

To make it seem like we are bolder

Feeling like there is a wall there

Though help can be found where

Looking for someone near

To stop hiding all of my fears

William Randy Parker Jr. - 17

Talking

You don't know how it will go

Just as long as you know

To get inside a persons mind

To see what's going on inside

Just to hear that person's voice

Makes my heart rejoice

For she knows how happy she makes me

With her love it will never forsake me

A Good Woman

Doesn't have to be a certain way

What will make her come to you and say?

Its like a dream comes true

Cause all I do my...I miss you

Thinking about you all the time

Wondering about when the next time I see you will come by

Such a very good heart you have

I would like to say I love you on my behalf

William Randy Parker Jr. - 19

Rose Petals

Just to have you walk into the room

Without any words spoken to you

To sit you down

Have you look around

Have your favorite color

Layed out on the bed in front of you

Not knowing where to start

But let me first say you are my heart

Hear From You

Can't wait to I hear your voice

My heart has no choice

Your voice alone brightens up my day

That is why I don't like want your away

Thinking about what you are doing

As my heart can't sit still and keeps on moving

Waiting for the time to come

Her voice I will hear from

Picking You Up

There is nothing like seeing you

Cause I always want to be with you

Smiling from ear to ear

Cause I know she is almost near

Never wanting to let go

That's why my love for her will always show

She knows just what to say

To make me feel a certain way

Loving Her

It is the best thing in the world

To me she is the best girl

Told her close

Really means the most

Just to look into her eyes

Makes me not wonder why

As deep as my passion goes for her

I always can't wait to see her

Chocolate

Something that taste so good

Having you say I wish you would

Something that feels so good

Feels like it came from above

Will never get enough of it

Looking for her sweet love

Cause her love I will never get enough

Here love is so sweet

Cause her love knocks me to my feet

Going Home

A restful place to be

Sometimes I wish it were just me

To see one person again

Would make me so happy within

Haven't seen that person in awhile

Feel so much love seeing them smile

Wondering what that will be like

Cause this person had such an influence on my life

William Randy Parker Jr. - 25

Waffle Cone Ice Cream

Just one taste

Can really blow you away

Just to see your expression

For you to eat it before it starts melting

If it looks this good

I wonder if I should

She is thinking what to do

I'm wondering if I should kiss you

Just The Way You Are

Love is in the air

With so much to share

Walking the street

Looking for her for my heart to beat

Spending time with her

Always have to show how much I missed her

Loving her always

Cause in my heart she is never far away

Numbers

They can go up

Whenever you show up

Sometimes you have to subtract

Then when the time is right will it come back?

I am good with this one person

Cause my love for her multiplied

She is the best woman on the inside

Happy that she is by my side

Cause she will always be mine

Taking Control

I want to see what you can do

Cause you know that I have missed you

Thinking of all the things

Makes my mind start to sing

Just the thought of you

That's why I always say I can't wait to see you

Mind blowing expressions

Of not knowing what's going on within

Delivery

One day it will be

A couple additions to you and me

To make both of us smile

While we love them all the while

Telling them our love with much to stay

But deliver it to em in a nice way

To look into this woman's eyes

Our children will be giving so much love from inside

Love Of My Life

I prayed

That someone would come my way

She makes me feel a certain way

I don't like it when she is away

Just to hear her say

That I am on the way

I can't wait for the time to display

She knows I love her a certain way

Love of my life she always stays

Laying Beside You

Its like nothing else matters

Not wanting anything else to happen

Looking into her eyes

Not wanting to leave her side

Time goes by to fast

When I have you in my arms I want it to last

As the music plays on

My love for you will always continue on

Instrumental

No words

Can be heard

The beat sounds so sweet

That will knock you off your feet

Can you really think?

So you better not blink

Pen to pad

I see you as all I have

My Thoughts

I want to keep them in a vault

Cause I don't know where to start

Expressions can last

Cause of something you always had

A foot down on the payment…is it really meant?

I say that you were heaven sent

As I write them down

I know whom I will always be around

If I Could

Life would be so much better

If I could tell them

What is on my mind?

At any giving time

Feeling always on the run

She has my heart without reason

To see everything go away

Cause this one person has come my way

Am I On

Feeling already gone

Feeling like I stole home

No time to roam

Cause my mind is blown

Cause of what's going on

Bad days are gone

Cause I am not alone

Cause my heart is not gone

On Pace

Feels like this is a race

Worried about this place

Or what may come this way

Mouth open and wanting to say

To have something to display

Cause when she has something to say

Takes her some time to come this way

Cause I am looking for something to make its way

A New Day

Taking a breath

Not knowing if I will need some help

Wondering when I will see her

Cause I really need her

She sounds so sweet

I can't wait for our bodies to meet

As the sun goes up and down

My love lost has been found

Did We Meet

Remember a face

Just by a certain way

Looking down the line

How the mind flashes back in rewind

Something about your face

I know we met at this place

I look forward to catching up with you

Cause I know that I have really missed you

Right Next Door

Can't believe you are so close

Makes me want you more

To be able to walk into the next room

To be able to just look at you

To see the smile on my girl

To me that means the world

Holding on to you tight

Keeping you right in my sight

Instrumentals Pt. 2

So much drama has come

From one song

I know my heart was wrong

But please come home

Looking into the window

I see I really miss you

Breaking it all down

I don't know where is the sound

All the love

My brain feels frozen

From all the love within

Going on day by day

What made my heart stay?

I look up to the sky

Not to wonder why

Not feeling ashamed

Where is the right side of my brain?

Crazy

This is about to drive me insane

Losing my baby from this pain

Praying that it will rain

Most feelings stay the same

No games

But to remain the same

As the heart pounds

I still wonder where is the sound

Walk To Me

Looking for her to walk to me

Wondering will she kiss me

Writing down my thoughts

Not even wanting to walk

Driving up close to the door

Leave me wanting so much more

I Am

Fortunate that I am

To see whom I really am

Past the breaking points

This one I want for sure

I envision her love

Cause it was sent from above

Thoughts

Rolling on with these thoughts

I pray that I left my mark

As time continue to go

She knows I will never go

As each time I look into her eyes

Its like time stands still and doesn't pass by

Always Stay

I want to always stay in her love

Cause she provides tough love

Roller-skating around her heart

She knows I love her with every drop

Tapping my foot on the floor

Knowing any minute she will mean more

Soon walking through the door

Mind Of Hers

Imagine laying beside her

Exploring the mind of hers

As the beat goes louder

My love for her will never go sour

You have every second, minute, and hour

Isn't any need to buy no vowels?

Passion

The passion that grows

Makes my love for you run even more

Turning you back around

You are the reason my heart makes sound

I was alone

But I thank God you came along

In Me

Everybody seems

What you believe in me

It's hard to say

But they are happy for me they say

As the beat continues to play

This is something I have to say

Write About It

To bottom out
Without a bout
Shaking my head
Cause to lay in the bed
Rest my head on your shoulders
Before you hold and fold them
With the stars shining so bright

One Love

Where our love come from

Love is a process from some

That's why I am proud of us

Cause to me you mean the most

Love doesn't know when it will happen

Cause my love has found your love and now it not sadden

To You

Snapping my fingers

What does this really mean to me

Expressions of love

Can I shower her from above?

Wake up right next to her

Just to give her a big ole hug

Down

Loving her down

Cause she is the only one

That I always want to hear from

I am not going to run

Cause her body is the one

Always will be my heart

Cause she has been the best from the start

Stories

Waiting for it to start

Wondering if saying it will be smart

Tale of two stories

But both have been placed before me

They can came at the at the wrong time

But will everything be fine

In due time

What is on your mind?

Once Before

Has it happen

That makes you feel sad within

Looking to feel comfortable

But inside I feel horrible

The talk of the town

When there is no one around

Is this something you can write about?

Without having any doubts

How Do You See

A reflection of me

Can only be seen

Living in the shadows

But why are you and though

Feeling the pressures of everyday

So many things will make you say

But will you be the one to walk away

William Randy Parker Jr. - 57

Why?

A good question to ask

But will that answer last

Could it be about something that work?

Will you try to make it work?

Hands up and hands down

To many things going around

What would life be without sound?

Photograph

Holding on to something

When life feels bumpy

All the good times

Align them in a line

If they could speak to you

Would you want them to tell you the truth?

Away

Some say it is the best

When you can rest

Eyes looking tired

But the body feeling wired

If I could talk to you

To see only what you knew

New Message

When the phone alerts

What will you do first?

Will you write back?

To tell them where you are

Reading it is all you can do

Next best thing when I am unable to see you

A Certain Spot

To put something on it

Wondering if it could just sit

Between the areas

Might even be unheard of

What can be seen from above?

Would you tell the person where you are going?

Without even showing

A Gift

When will it be sent?

Is it, will it be meant?

As the days come and go

I know where I will always let my words show

I am the same person

But why am I hurting?

Write it down

See when I will come around

A Hug

Sure could use one

A lot more than one

Stress

Seems to be a big test to ease the pain

Of so many things

To be in that one persons arms

Cause there love is so strong

Friendship

What does the word really mean?

Some people aren't who they seem

Some just saying anything

Not carrying if they really mean

Breaking it all down

Would you really want to be around?

Life brings so many ifs

So what is the word friendship?

When You See Me

What will you do?

When you see me walking up to you

I'm so in love

Cause I am glad of what she does

Already to see

What will be?

Having her in my arms

Cause the thoughts I write down are for her alone

Thrown

Feels like my heart is going in circles

Feels like my heart has turned from red to purple

Feels like I am out of it

Feels like I am about to have a fit

Feels like she doesn't know

Feels like I want to show

Feels like a new day

Feels like you will come my way

Tears

Holding you last night

I didn't want to let you out my sight

Your touch felt so good

I wish I could

Not knowing what you want to do

Still remains there is no issue

Dream has come true

Cause I am laying right her next to you

On & Off

Where to begin

Cause to me your beyond a ten

Love is in the air

But with you I only share

What would happen if I kissed you there?

Would it make your heart melt somewhere?

Will I find out if you come over here?

Sleeper

Not feeling very good

With you I wish I could

Not long before you go

But you know I will miss you more

Not wanting to bother you

But not wanting to what you go through

I hope you are not a sleeper are you

Blank Expressions

Not knowing to say

Will I even want to walk that way?

Though so much has happen

Why do I feel sadden?

I have seen so much

Not willing to give it up

Cold

Needing to feel warm

To be in someone's arms

Looking for my best friend

To be there til the end

Sunrise to sun down

Will they be around?

Be there to listen when I make a sound

Make It Happen

Will that day come?

Or will I still be on the run

To look at all the pages

What is being made of them?

Looking for a smile

There's one thing that has style

Getting Close

Feeling like no other

Nothing ever heard of

Something to leave you speechless

Not looking for any rest

A cut above all the rest

To me she is the best

Cause I am lost in her love nest

Taco Bell

One favorite place to go

Cause we both know

We can eat our butts off

Not even get in a word to talk

Just to see you smile

Cause you got that kind of style

William Randy Parker Jr. - 75

Together

Such a powerful word

When it is heard

Means two belong as one

So much love is upon

Going in to detail

How will there love prevail?

Between them love is all well

Will I?

Will I be the man you want me to be?

Will I when you look at me?

Will I make it?

Will I shake it?

Will I be able to take it?

Will I be able to save it?

William Randy Parker Jr. - 77

Miss You

Think about you everyday

I wonder what I will say

To see your face again

Where did our last conversation end?

I want to know what you have been doing?

That has had me looking

Cry

Does it help ease the pain?

Or does it drive you insane

What do you feel?

Is it even real?

To the point of no return

Where has life for you taken a turn

William Randy Parker Jr. - 79

Decisions

Such a key word

But you are the only one being heard

Can go right or wrong

In the end will you be alone

Your choice will stick with you

But can your heart ever forgive you

What will you do?

Behind

Getting caught up

Trying to make a buck

Information goes around

Just like the talk of the town

Feeling pressed

You just feel like there is no time for rest

Stand By Me

It's all I want to do
Is know that I am with you
Whatever we go through
I know it will be with you
Looking down the line
I can see what on my mind

Respect

Is it something you earn?

Is it something that makes your stomach churn?

How do people see you?

When they introduce you

Would you do something?

Not to tell them and go alone

Could It Be

Do I have a reason?

What is the reason?

No one sight

No reason to put up a fight

To be proud of how things are

Look how far they came where you are

Stars

They shine so bright

They look like they our out of sight

Holding on to your dreams

To make them become your reality

Someone up in the sky

There is someone saying hi

William Randy Parker Jr. - 85

Limitations

Is there any to have

How long will it last?

You make me forget about my past

Cause you the best I ever had

With you the best I ever had

With you I know I can handle any task

As I write my feelings to you on this pad

Going For It

Feeling like nothing else is left

This is no help

Going on my on

Have to get past singing this song

So much emotion

Why have it showing

William Randy Parker Jr. - 87

Too Late

What's done is done

Don't try to run

Cause it will not be fun

My love for you has begun

You have reached the point of no return

I will stop when I am done

For only this has just begun

Test Of Times

Will she be mine?

I wonder in time

As time counts down

I will not make a sound

She is all I ever needed

To be treated

William Randy Parker Jr. - 89

Hard Print

Can tell so many things

About what you bring

Heart of gold

How is your story told?

Will you say it right?

Without having to put up a fight

As the band plays on

Where did we go wrong?

Soft

Toss you in the air

But where

So scared

Will you be there?

Sitting somewhere

There is a pair

William Randy Parker Jr. - 91

Finish

When you have done

To how what was won

Making light

Of what's right

Tonight's the night

That I will prove you right

Hold my hand

You will understand

Pain

Can come in many ways

Some to make you say

I will gone and walk the other way

And you will not hear me say

That I am okay

Though the pain will go away

You words will always stay

Cause my heart is no longer for yours to play

William Randy Parker Jr. - 93

People

Will do anything

Because the are saying

Test of time

What's going on the inside?

Will they show themselves?

Without something being felt

Down and down again

I remain myself within

Apology

When is it time…to be the right time?

When you know you are wrong on the inside

Will you even say anything?

Cause you know how they are feeling

To touch that persons heart

That is where to start

Letting it all out

Without having to shout

William Randy Parker Jr. - 95

Hear From Me

Don't know when the next time

I will have you by my side

Just know you are on my mind

Every second of time

I am dedicated fully

Cause your heart moves with me

Call You

Can't wait to hear from you

Cause how much I miss you

Such a beautiful voice when she speaks

It makes me weak

I look forward to it all the time

Cause I am fortunate you are mine

William Randy Parker Jr. - 97

All Of You

I want it all the time

You stay on my mind

On my right side

I will not hide

To love you on the inside

Gives me a piece of pride

That I got the right woman by my side

Amazing

She is the best person I ever known

She got me to her own

She is always there

To let me know she really cares

I am lost in her love

She is the best I could ever ask of

William Randy Parker Jr. - 99

Celebration

Every time I see you

It's like fireworks with you

I clap my hand

For you to understand

I love you deeply and dearly

Always love you near me

I want to spend the life I have with you

Cause there is no celebration without you

Taking The Time

Taking the time to look around

Wondering how to be found

Through all the pain and the struggle

You find some way to let nothing hold you

Holding your head up to the sky

You see your friends go by and by

Staying true to how you are

No matter how far you are

Though so many things may change

Loyalty and love remains the same

challenges are often brought about

That can make you say how did this come about

On this road through life

There are a lot of bumps in sight

Snuggles

Yeah this world right here is what I have

It is like the word was sent from above

She is everything I ever wanted

That's why I call her mom

She shuts it down

Because she makes her own sound

On My Mind

There's never a minute that goes by

When you are not on my mind

Thinking of my baby

How I wish she was with me

To have her is an honor

My love is upon her

I Will Be

Only time will tell

What life spells

To take this journey

To see what will be put before me

One day have a big smile

For I know I will go that extra mile

Holding on tight

Because I believe something is in sight

Open

To be able to speak

Not to worry about being neat

Expressions from the heart

Tell you where to start

To open up

Can reveal some stuff

But I will be here

So there is no need to be still

A Fantasy

Something you want to happen

Over and over again

To make it from place to place

Not knowing what to say

All is up in the air

But you know where

Take it to the next level

But I don't want to cause trouble

Come This Way

I wondered if it will ever happen

To stop feeling sad within

Something that looks so good

Make you say I wish you would

The best thing that has ever happen

That has made me better within

My heart beats faster

Because now I have her

Close Minded

So many things to say

But something gets in the way

You know there is something to get out

That can bring on a lot of doubt

What brings on a lot of pain

Something that will drive you insane

But it is something that will be found

That love is around

Everything

Means everything to you

With no issues

Can't wait to see them

Look into there eyes

See what can arise

What Was Said

Can throw you off

But what comes out of your mouth

Can hit hard

Just little words by far

Make you wonder why

To see tears in my eyes

Hurts for a little while

When they tell you because I am not with you

Timeless

Head on the pillow

Feeling shallow

Nowhere to go

I say to myself hello

Where to go see

What life means

What could happen

To not feel sad within

Long Road

I may not be the best

But I have passed my test

My emotions get the best of me

But I remain me

Tired yes some days

But I still make a way

Burning down my troubles

Feel like I seen that long road before

Fireball

Something that is red

Not being said

Something that comes fast

Hopefully it will last

Looking for an escape path

From the things that make you sad

Not knowing how fast

You might just run past

Thoughts

Could be about anything

In the form of many things

Could it be a dream

Of something that could seem

As the clock ticks on

I think about it so on and so on

Thought process

But you wonder where it will rest

Can You Be

There is a question
That has been placed before me
Spilling all my thoughts out
So you can see what I am about
Understanding my role
So what I know
There is a time and a place
There I know my love will stay

Flipping Papers

Trying to find an answer

Far from where I stand from

Holding on tight

To see what is in my sight

Putting in work

What is written all over your shirt

On and on I say

I'm tired of feeling this way

Burning Passion

What is this feeling

Like something hit the ceiling

Away from it all

Make a problem seem so small

Turning around and around

I would like to be found

What is passion

Does it come from within

Decisions

The hardest thing in life

Can come with a price

One word

Is all it takes to be heard

Open your eyes

To see whats right by your side

Somethings never change

But you always wonder who will remain the same

A Bottle

What can it contain

Bu looking at the contents of its frame

What is the color

What does it do for you

Sticking to the play

Just by looking at it you don't know what to say

You see the water going down

The coolness is on a meltdown

Breaking Down

When you feel like no one is around

Not even a person around town

Close enough to see To grab the keys

Wanting to know what it is

To say there it is

The ability to bring yourself back up

Is to look at yourself and say wake up

Good Days

Can never have enough of them

Since starting when

Appreciating the good things

Love that can be shared between

Stepping out into the world

Like a new born being held

You can smile the whole day

Because everything is going your way

Lines

They can go in a lot of ways

They have a story to say

What you have been through

Fitting through the issues

Being battles tested

Without even knowing what test it is

A sense of direction

To see where love falls within

Around The World

Would be a journey

Picture this for me

Stopping to think

But my mind draws a blank

A photo can mean a thousand words

But just by looking at it what can be heard

Speaking in the box

My love will never stop

Waiting

For the next time I will see you

To have your body in front of me

I want to take you so high

That it never feels like we say goodbye

Daddy will always be by your side

Daddy's Girl

Something that is one of a kind

She is always on my mind

She is very smart

I have loved her from the start

I tell her I love her

Because I adore her

William Randy Parker Jr. - 125

Beautiful

Just someone that I love a lot

My mind is always on the clock

Thinking of all the beautiful things

How she makes my heart sing

I want to hold her

She is the love I never had before

Ready To See You

I'm always ready to come see you

Because I have really missed you

I have a heart full of love

She was sent to me from above

I want to shower her

Just like the rain that comes from above

My Number 1 Girl

She is so important to me

Cause she has been there for me

So much has happen

That love has come back within

The love of my life

She always knows how to make things right

Expressing that I love her

She is my number 1 for sure

Time Away

I don't know what to do

Because I really miss you

Looking for you

Is the hardest thing to do

I don't even know what to say

Because I want so bad for my girl to stay

The Bestor

She is everything and more

Everything I hoped for

I've waited so long

To have you in my arms

You are the woman of my dreams

I love you with everything

No one will or can replace you

Because I am nothing without you

Frozen

Feels like time stops

When I see you walk

My love flows for you

Everyday I miss you

I feel so cold when I am alone

Because my baby is gone

It feels like daddy can't go home

But he will stand til it is time to go home

Tell Me

What is on your mind

To see what is going on the inside

How do you feel?

To keep it 100 percent real

Look into your eyes

Just to make your should cry

Ready to let go

I will always be there to hold

Everything

Means so much

Just by her touch

She much she has done

She has stopped my love from running

She has takin a journey

That has been placed before me

Letting her know

That she has made me whole

Touch On It

Just to see how you will get

When my hands go in

Having you right there

With all the passion in the air

To see how it makes you feel

Just by having me near

So soft is all I can say

That's my baby all the way

Amen

She has brought me so much joy

So much love to behold

I look in the sky

Say there my baby in my eyes

I chose her to love

Because she keeps me above

First of love to be real love

From someone that provides hugs

Process

How long does it take to love

With whats right above

When time is takin away

How do you know what to say

Wondering when it will be time to go

Because she knows

It was a long time coming

Never imagined something before me

To wrap my arms around you

Let you know that I missed you

Promise Ring

To sit here and thing about all the things

About what you mean to me

To hold your hands in my heart

You have had me from the start

To look into your eyes

It feels like I have been on a long ride

My Imagination goes for with you

Cause I feel I am nothing without you

Imagination

I feel like we can go as far as we want to

I feel that as long as I am with you

To hold you tightly

I love having you right beside me

You alone have brought so much out of me

That my love for you fights constantly

Rain Drops

When they fall from the sky

I sometimes wonder why

If a drop told a story

I wonder which one part brought you before me

The sound that each drop makes

Feels like my baby is coming towards this way

Holding on to each moment

How much love you have shown on it

Happiness

It describes you

How much I want to be with you

You alone have changed everything in my life

That is why it feels so right

As precious as you are

You are my shining star

With everything that happens

There is no limit for that love I have for you within

Touching

To feel your smooth body is amazing

To feel my hands move through your skin

Never have I felt something so great

That allows me to not hesitate

My heart just stops

When there is time for my hands to walk

Gently moving my hands through your body

Something about you keeps me reminding me

Colors

Could mean a variety of things

Of what could be something in between

Something that can be heartfelt

Can just be a color to make the heart melt

Just thought of it

The love from you I get

Just having you by my side

I know I have the best prize

Laying There

Just looking at someone while they lay

Can cause a relaxation without delay

To do something to surprise them

To know that you can confide in them

Thinking of something to say

About how they make you feel a certain way

Without delay

You know that I will always be there to stay

Love Stays

No matter what happens

The road to your love is where I'm in

All the things that are said

Traveling through my heart and into your head

Expressions that come from the face

Will never be disgraced

Because you are my favorite lady

And I pray that you will always stay baby

Pen To Pad

I wonder where my words will go

Just to let someone know

That I am always there

To let her know I am near

Breaking down the bad thoughts

To see whats in someone's heart

Knowing day to day

I can say there goes my baby

Where I Want To Be

Is to always be with you

Because I always miss you

Not a minute goes by

When you are not on my mind

You are so important to me

There is so much I want to see

Endless time with you I want to spend

I love you so much from within

Heaven

I thank God that I have found you

To wonder when I can kiss you

As my heart continues to beat

I stand to my feet when I see you in front of me

How a person can have so much love

That was sent to him from above

I wish you were here

To feel what I feel

My World

You mean so much to me

Because you have stuck with me

Turning the page

From what has been made

My heart is finally open

So that I can put everything all in

To be seen as the best person I can be

Only with you I know I want to be

You Alone

I will always be there

To let you know I care

Through everything you remain the same

Never scared to say

My mind never goes far away

Because I know where my heart stays

Wondering about the future

Is there anything I can do for you

Looking for the center lane

Because my love for you will always remain the same

Miss You

Two powerful words

That I love you being heard

Just to brighten up your day

The perfect words to say

I wonder how it makes you feel?

That what I feel in my heart is real

Everyday is a new journey

To know that you are here for me

Hanging on to your love

Because I believe you were sent from above

Spend My Life With You

Every day I wonder what it would be like

To have you always in my sight

To come home with you

To tell you how much I missed you

Over time we have grown

When you are not around I feel alone

To be able to look at you every night

To say snuggles is right in my sight

Beautiful

The one word that describes you

Anything I can do for you I will

To look into your eyes

Feels like love is going on deep inside

Having you right in front of me

Leave me speechless on how beautiful you are to me

As time passes on

My shoulder you can always come lean on

I'm so glad I have you

Because to me you are so beautiful

Holding On

As the world turns

Feels like you can sometimes be on the run

So many thoughts

So many battles fought

Wondering what will be next

You know you can pass any test

Shooting for the stars

Because you know who you are Through it all

I will not let you fall

Understand

Looking at what brought this on

Will I be able to walk alone

Looking at the footsteps I need to take

In order to hold up my head

To know that I can run

From thing that are not fun

To be able to look at myself

Know that I have help

Putting my thoughts down

Without making a sound

Something To Me

Means so much

Without that persons touch

I don't know where to begin

All this love I have for her within

Going on day by day

I think about her all day

She mean so much to me

I make sure she will hear it from me

Holding on to her so tight

My hearts gets out and fights

William Randy Parker Jr. - 155

Pepsi

It's my girls favorite drink

Without having even to think

Just mention that word

She gone make sure it gets heard

It just makes her so happy

To have that P.E.P.S.I.

To see her smile when she drinks one

Just makes me say hum hum....hum

Songs

Can set the mood

To wonder what could

Understanding what could take place

As your heart continues to race

Wondering what she will say

Just as soon as she presses play

Can put your mind at ease

Have the track on repeat

To know that is is real

About what she feels

Always Forever

I promise to remain the same

To tell you what I mean

To just thank about you baby

How you are always there for me

We are in love

I believe you were sent to me from above

I will never leave

Because you are someone I need

I will be yours

I will always be with you and this is for sure

One Of A Kind

Your always on my mind

At any giving moment of time

I look to you as a wonderful woman

To you I have a lot of love within

I know you are the one for me

Because of all the things you have showed me

When my heart beats

You are where I want to be

I couldn't tell you how much you mean to me

Because without you there would be no me

You have made me a better person

I found the love that I have been searchin

Up To You

Baby I belong to you

Because of how much I love and miss you

Nothing in this world will take me away from you

Because I always miss you

I am so in love with you

I think about all we can do

Thinking of your beautiful smile

How my mind thinks of you all this while

I couldn't tell you how much I love you

That's why I still get nervous when I stand before you

I want to spend the rest of my life with you

Because you are the woman that has made my dreams come true

Have No Fear

Mrs. Strawberry have no fear

My love will always be right here

As each day goes by

My love for you never dies

My heart beats so much love for you

That is why I can't wait to be with you

You are very important to me

Looking into your eyes

There is no reason for me to wonder why

So many people can see what you mean to me

Because they see a different person now that you are with me

My heart, mind, body, and soul

It is all yours for only you to hold

Me

What can I say

This is who I portray

Always thought to be a good person

Words keep me straight within

Holding on to what people see me as

Not letting life pass

I have some bruises

Your life is all I need it sure is

Thoughts going through my head

Of how wonderful Mrs. Strawberry is

I hope and pray by her reading this

She will know how deep my love for her really is

Standing Here

All that has happen today

Nothing seems to be going the right way

I let my words come through this pen

Letting the world know how I feel within

Going through this journey today

All I could think about is a special lady

She had a lot on her mind

But just enough time

I tell her how much she means to me

Not knowing the next time she will see me

Always in my heart

This girls love is always with me from the start

Moment For Life

A moment for life

To have whatever you like

I have written down

Wanting not to be found

Feeling a long way gone

Where to call home

In my heart you will always stay

To ask if I may

Thinking of a certain person

That I am always certain

Wondering how she feels

How beautiful she is

As each day comes along

In my heart there is a song

It beats for her only

Because my heart she stole from me

To have and to hold

As we roll

Day Comes Around

When the day comes around

She knows that I will be around

As I look around

Her happiness makes a sound

I will forever be happy

That she has lifted the sadness from me

As the beat plays along

My love for her will only go on

Not stuck in my ways

But this girl I say

She is my everything

Hope to provide that one thing

I am who I am

To be able to take a stand

Breathing easy now

She is my sound

I love her with all my heart

I have from the start

Sight

Because I will not go down without a fight

Holding my head high

To be in the right state of mind

Not to sleep on my dreams

To write down what I have seen

Going down the road to see

That here love is all I really need

She said take my hand

Because we will always stand

Building on her love

Is the best thing of all

To be wanted by someone

That love will always go on

Being able to call you my own

Is what I have been wanting to do for so long

Never looking to make a mistake

I will our love at stake

Holding on very tight

To let you know I will always be in your sight

All Of Me

Giving my all

Our love with never fall

True love being put on

Telling the pain so long

Thinking about all these thoughts

Seeing how we have come by far

Day in and day out

You are all I think about

Seeing this beautiful woman

That is sure of me

Every time I see her

I love to be near her

Time away from her

My heart is not sure of

Waiting on this day

For something I would love to say

Special To Me

She is very special to me

All I want to see

To look into her eyes

I get lost all on the inside

She is the best person I ever known

Because I have her as my own

Holding her is like a dream come true

Because I always want to show you how much I missed you

Being Found

I have found the woman of my life

Because I always want to stay on her right side

She has changed so much in my life

On this special day

There is so passion for you in each and every way

This is not a dream

Because you mean so much to me

I know I will always love her

That is in my heart for sure

Writing down how I feel

Because the love I have for you is real

Take Me Away

Nothing can take me away

Because I am hooked on you and will always stay

Keeping it close

Between who means the most

Writing stuff down with so much passion

Her love is where it has been

Nothing else compares

Where you are in my world

What my eyes have seen

She feels that hole of whats been missing

Loving her mentally

Really does something to me

Learning every single day

About my ways

Will She Say

What will she say

If I am not a certain way

Breaking away from it all

To see what shall

Step into the light

But look for what is right

Love that continues to grow

All there is to say is behold

You are my heart

Been from the start

Having an escape

To go to your love a very safe place

William Randy Parker Jr. - 171

My Dream.....My Heart....My Lifetime

To say that I do not feel a certain way

With all that I would like to share

Wondering if any one would ever be there

This is why I believe my heart has truly found something

Day after day it means more and more to me

To be in your presence

I feel like the whole world stops before me

To be faithful and never hurt you

To look into your eyes and show you passion

Without a doubt you are very special to me

I am the luckiest man in the world

This beautiful woman is my girl

I feel like nothing else matters

Just the thought of her make my heart scatters

Letting you know how much you mean to me

From the top of my head all the way to the bottom of my feet

I can't imagine being with anyone else

You are truly priceless and you have my heart following your footsteps

Anytime

On top of you

love that is taking to another level

whenever I am with you

looking into your eyes

I know it will always be an amazing ride

the way you make me feel

it is beyond feeling unreal

the way you move your body

feels like you are flying

you feel so great

got always feeling like I never ate

you are the sweetest person I have ever known

yes it is true to the love we continue to make has grown

the passion is all about you

My Dream...My Heart...My Lifetime

To say that I do not feel a certain way

With all that I would like to share

Wondering if any one would ever be there

This is why I believe my heart has truly found something

Day after day it means more and more to me

To be in your presence

I feel like the whole world stops before me

To be faithful and never hurt you

To look into your eyes and you passion

Without a doubt you are very special to me

I am the luckiest man in the world

This beautiful woman is my girl

I feel like nothing else matters

Just the thought of her makes my heart scatter

Letting you know how much you mean to me

From the top of my head all the way down to the bottom of
my feet

I can't and won't imagine being with anyone else

You truly priceless and you have my heart following your
footsteps

About the Author

I am qualified to write this book because I speak solely from my heart and the experiences that I have gone through so far in life. The many trials and tribulations that I have endured have made me stronger as person on the inside as well as the outside. I express my feelings through writing because at the time I may not be feeling good but my words may help someone else feel better.

I am very quite person but i love to write about what is on my mind and how I feel about it. To me writing is it sense of relaxation and freedom because someone else to read what you wrote down and relate to it.

I currently live in North Carolina and I am a shy but nice person that love to make people laugh. Most importantly I just love to make people feel good about themselves just by what I write.